ihappy

ecological and egological

Nalle Windahl

First edition

Publisher: BoD - Books on Demand, Stockholm, Sweden
Printer: BoD - Books on Demand, Norderstedt, Germany

ISBN: 978-91-7969-350-3

Another book for you to fill in and challenge yourself to personal development. This time it is about you and the climate.

Perhaps you are wondering about the title, ecological and egological. What does it mean?

Well, the ecological part is hopefully self-explaining, it is about the planet, how to live sustainably in perspective of the planet and the future. Despite the nobility in that, I believe that one part of the perspective is missing.

Most agree that drastic measures are needed, right away, preferably yesterday. If not, we have no means to slow down or stop the climate changes. My point of view is that we also need to consider another perspective, namely the perspective of you and me. The egoistic perspective.

Egologic.

Whatever changes I (you) am prepared to make, in my (your) life, where I (you) feel that my (your) sacrifices are worth making. Where I (you) feel that I (you) can commit and sustain. Only then my (your) contribution and efforts will make actual changes that will affect the planet and environment.

I believe that what I am prepared to do might not be the same as what you are prepared to do, but I believe that we are both prepared to change things in our life to contribute. Perhaps not just the same things. Thus, whatever things you are prepared to change, change them, and I will do the same.

I hope you will find inspiration and pleasure in challenging yourself with this book! Enjoy!

^..^

The structure

Each part of this book is composed of five identical parts where you choose a topic to focus on. You choose the topic and as inspiration, here are some examples:

- How do I change my dietary habits to adjust to the climate change?
- How can I change my use of electricity?
- In what way can I improve my water consumption?
- What can I do to lower my food waste?
- How do I shop?
- What do I shop?
- Clothes - can I change anything in my wardrobe or the way I dress?
- Home electronics - what are my choices and my priorities?
- Transport - what can I do to lower my climate footprint?
- Travels - how and where do I choose to travel, what is it worth to me?
- New things or preloved, what are my thoughts on this?
- My home - what can I change in or around my home to lower my climate footprint?
- At work or in school, what improvements can I do here?

There is no right or wrong choice in regards to the topic, but the success rate is higher if you choose something you feel you can really commit to. And even if you have chosen one topic at one time, and you feel you have other perspectives, there is nothing wrong with revisiting that topic.

As you have worked with five topics, you find a section where you can reflect on two things:

- How do I expose myself to new and inspiring ideas to keep developing?
- How do I keep my current motivation?

Then it is time for five more.

The goal is to find sustainable changes in your life that you can commit to over time. Only then you can make changes that really matter to this planet and to our future.

Ecological and egological!

Now, go ahead, do your thing!

My topic:

_____

_____

_____

_____

_____

_____

_____

_____

_____

_____

_____

_____

_____

_____

_____

_____

What do I do today that I need to keep doing?

_____

_____

_____

_____

_____

_____

_____

_____

_____

_____

_____

_____

_____

_____

What do I do today that I need to stop doing?

_____

_____

_____

_____

_____

_____

_____

_____

_____

_____

_____

_____

_____

_____

What can I start to do today?

_____

_____

_____

_____

_____

_____

_____

_____

_____

_____

_____

_____

_____

My topic:

_____

_____

_____

_____

_____

_____

_____

_____

_____

_____

_____

_____

_____

_____

What do I do today that I need to keep doing?

_____

_____

_____

_____

_____

_____

_____

_____

_____

_____

_____

_____

_____

_____

What do I do today that I need to stop doing?

_____

_____

_____

_____

_____

_____

_____

_____

_____

_____

_____

_____

_____

_____

_____

What can I start to do today?

_____

_____

_____

_____

_____

_____

_____

_____

_____

_____

_____

_____

_____

My topic:

What do I do today that I need to keep doing?

_____

_____

_____

_____

_____

_____

_____

_____

_____

_____

_____

_____

_____

What do I do today that I need to stop doing?

_____

_____

_____

_____

_____

_____

_____

_____

_____

_____

_____

_____

_____

_____

What can I start to do today?

_____

_____

_____

_____

_____

_____

_____

_____

_____

_____

_____

_____

_____

_____

My topic:

_____

_____

_____

_____

_____

_____

_____

_____

_____

_____

_____

_____

_____

_____

What do I do today that I need to keep doing?

_____

_____

_____

_____

_____

_____

_____

_____

_____

_____

_____

_____

_____

What do I do today that I need to stop doing?

_____

_____

_____

_____

_____

_____

_____

_____

_____

_____

_____

_____

_____

_____

What can I start to do today?

_____

_____

_____

_____

_____

_____

_____

_____

_____

_____

_____

_____

_____

My topic:

_____

_____

_____

_____

_____

_____

_____

_____

_____

_____

_____

_____

_____

_____

_____

_____

What do I do today that I need to keep doing?

_____

_____

_____

_____

_____

_____

_____

_____

_____

_____

_____

_____

_____

_____

What do I do today that I need to stop doing?

_____

_____

_____

_____

_____

_____

_____

_____

_____

_____

_____

_____

_____

_____

What can I start to do today?

_____

_____

_____

_____

_____

_____

_____

_____

_____

_____

_____

_____

_____

_____

Reflection: How do I expose myself to new and inspiring ideas to keep developing?

_____

_____

_____

_____

_____

_____

_____

_____

_____

_____

_____

_____

Reflection: How do I keep my current motivation?

My topic:

_____

_____

_____

_____

_____

_____

_____

_____

_____

_____

_____

_____

_____

_____

What do I do today that I need to keep doing?

_____

_____

_____

_____

_____

_____

_____

_____

_____

_____

_____

_____

_____

What do I do today that I need to stop doing?

_____

_____

_____

_____

_____

_____

_____

_____

_____

_____

_____

_____

_____

_____

What can I start to do today?

_____

_____

_____

_____

_____

_____

_____

_____

_____

_____

_____

_____

_____

My topic:

_____

_____

_____

_____

_____

_____

_____

_____

_____

_____

_____

_____

_____

_____

What do I do today that I need to keep doing?

_____

_____

_____

_____

_____

_____

_____

_____

_____

_____

_____

_____

_____

What do I do today that I need to stop doing?

_____

_____

_____

_____

_____

_____

_____

_____

_____

_____

_____

_____

_____

What can I start to do today?

_____

_____

_____

_____

_____

_____

_____

_____

_____

_____

_____

_____

_____

My topic:

_____

_____

_____

_____

_____

_____

_____

_____

_____

_____

_____

_____

_____

What do I do today that I need to keep doing?

_____

_____

_____

_____

_____

_____

_____

_____

_____

_____

_____

_____

_____

What do I do today that I need to stop doing?

_____

_____

_____

_____

_____

_____

_____

_____

_____

_____

_____

_____

_____

_____

What can I start to do today?

_____

_____

_____

_____

_____

_____

_____

_____

_____

_____

_____

_____

_____

My topic:

_____

_____

_____

_____

_____

_____

_____

_____

_____

_____

_____

_____

_____

_____

What do I do today that I need to keep doing?

_____

_____

_____

_____

_____

_____

_____

_____

_____

_____

_____

_____

_____

What do I do today that I need to stop doing?

_____

_____

_____

_____

_____

_____

_____

_____

_____

_____

_____

_____

_____

_____

What can I start to do today?

_____

_____

_____

_____

_____

_____

_____

_____

_____

_____

_____

_____

_____

My topic:

_____

_____

_____

_____

_____

_____

_____

_____

_____

_____

_____

_____

_____

_____

_____

What do I do today that I need to keep doing?

What do I do today that I need to stop doing?

_____

_____

_____

_____

_____

_____

_____

_____

_____

_____

_____

_____

_____

What can I start to do today?

_____

_____

_____

_____

_____

_____

_____

_____

_____

_____

_____

_____

_____

Reflection: How do I expose myself to new and inspiring ideas to keep developing?

_____

_____

_____

_____

_____

_____

_____

_____

_____

_____

_____

_____

Reflection: How do I keep my current motivation?

_____

_____

_____

_____

_____

_____

_____

_____

_____

_____

_____

_____

_____

My topic:

_____

_____

_____

_____

_____

_____

_____

_____

_____

_____

_____

_____

_____

_____

_____

_____

_____

What do I do today that I need to keep doing?

_____

_____

_____

_____

_____

_____

_____

_____

_____

_____

_____

_____

_____

What do I do today that I need to stop doing?

_____

_____

_____

_____

_____

_____

_____

_____

_____

_____

_____

_____

_____

_____

What can I start to do today?

_____

_____

_____

_____

_____

_____

_____

_____

_____

_____

_____

_____

_____

_____

My topic:

_____

_____

_____

_____

_____

_____

_____

_____

_____

_____

_____

_____

_____

_____

_____

_____

What do I do today that I need to keep doing?

_____

_____

_____

_____

_____

_____

_____

_____

_____

_____

_____

_____

_____

What do I do today that I need to stop doing?

_____

_____

_____

_____

_____

_____

_____

_____

_____

_____

_____

_____

_____

_____

What can I start to do today?

_____

_____

_____

_____

_____

_____

_____

_____

_____

_____

_____

_____

_____

_____

My topic:

What do I do today that I need to keep doing?

_____

_____

_____

_____

_____

_____

_____

_____

_____

_____

_____

_____

_____

_____

What do I do today that I need to stop doing?

_____

_____

_____

_____

_____

_____

_____

_____

_____

_____

_____

_____

_____

_____

_____

What can I start to do today?

_____

_____

_____

_____

_____

_____

_____

_____

_____

_____

_____

_____

_____

My topic:

_____

_____

_____

_____

_____

_____

_____

_____

_____

_____

_____

_____

_____

_____

_____

_____

_____

What do I do today that I need to keep doing?

What do I do today that I need to stop doing?

_____

_____

_____

_____

_____

_____

_____

_____

_____

_____

_____

_____

_____

What can I start to do today?

_____

_____

_____

_____

_____

_____

_____

_____

_____

_____

_____

_____

_____

My topic:

_____

_____

_____

_____

_____

_____

_____

_____

_____

_____

_____

_____

_____

_____

What do I do today that I need to keep doing?

_____

_____

_____

_____

_____

_____

_____

_____

_____

_____

_____

_____

_____

_____

What do I do today that I need to stop doing?

_____

_____

_____

_____

_____

_____

_____

_____

_____

_____

_____

_____

_____

_____

_____

What can I start to do today?

_____

_____

_____

_____

_____

_____

_____

_____

_____

_____

_____

_____

Reflection: How do I expose myself to new and inspiring ideas to keep developing?

_____

_____

_____

_____

_____

_____

_____

_____

_____

_____

_____

_____

Reflection: How do I keep my current motivation?

_____

_____

_____

_____

_____

_____

_____

_____

_____

_____

_____

_____

_____

My topic:

_____

_____

_____

_____

_____

_____

_____

_____

_____

_____

_____

_____

_____

_____

_____

What do I do today that I need to keep doing?

_____

_____

_____

_____

_____

_____

_____

_____

_____

_____

_____

_____

_____

What do I do today that I need to stop doing?

_____

_____

_____

_____

_____

_____

_____

_____

_____

_____

_____

_____

_____

_____

What can I start to do today?

_____

_____

_____

_____

_____

_____

_____

_____

_____

_____

_____

_____

_____

My topic:

What do I do today that I need to keep doing?

_____

_____

_____

_____

_____

_____

_____

_____

_____

_____

_____

_____

_____

What do I do today that I need to stop doing?

_____

_____

_____

_____

_____

_____

_____

_____

_____

_____

_____

_____

_____

What can I start to do today?

My topic:

_____

_____

_____

_____

_____

_____

_____

_____

_____

_____

_____

_____

_____

_____

_____

What do I do today that I need to keep doing?

_____

_____

_____

_____

_____

_____

_____

_____

_____

_____

_____

_____

What do I do today that I need to stop doing?

_____

_____

_____

_____

_____

_____

_____

_____

_____

_____

_____

_____

_____

_____

What can I start to do today?

_____

_____

_____

_____

_____

_____

_____

_____

_____

_____

_____

_____

_____

_____

My topic:

_____

_____

_____

_____

_____

_____

_____

_____

_____

_____

_____

_____

_____

What do I do today that I need to keep doing?

_____

_____

_____

_____

_____

_____

_____

_____

_____

_____

_____

_____

_____

What do I do today that I need to stop doing?

_____

_____

_____

_____

_____

_____

_____

_____

_____

_____

_____

_____

_____

_____

What can I start to do today?

_____

_____

_____

_____

_____

_____

_____

_____

_____

_____

_____

_____

_____

My topic:

_____

_____

_____

_____

_____

_____

_____

_____

_____

_____

_____

_____

_____

_____

What do I do today that I need to keep doing?

_____

_____

_____

_____

_____

_____

_____

_____

_____

_____

_____

_____

_____

What do I do today that I need to stop doing?

_____

_____

_____

_____

_____

_____

_____

_____

_____

_____

_____

_____

_____

_____

What can I start to do today?

_____

_____

_____

_____

_____

_____

_____

_____

_____

_____

_____

_____

_____

Reflection: How do I expose myself to new and inspiring ideas to keep developing?

_____

_____

_____

_____

_____

_____

_____

_____

_____

_____

_____

_____

Reflection: How do I keep my current motivation?

_____

_____

_____

_____

_____

_____

_____

_____

_____

_____

_____

_____

_____

_____

My topic:

_____

_____

_____

_____

_____

_____

_____

_____

_____

_____

_____

_____

_____

_____

What do I do today that I need to keep doing?

_____

_____

_____

_____

_____

_____

_____

_____

_____

_____

_____

_____

_____

What do I do today that I need to stop doing?

What can I start to do today?

My topic:

_____

_____

_____

_____

_____

_____

_____

_____

_____

_____

_____

_____

_____

_____

What do I do today that I need to keep doing?

_____

_____

_____

_____

_____

_____

_____

_____

_____

_____

_____

_____

What do I do today that I need to stop doing?

_____

_____

_____

_____

_____

_____

_____

_____

_____

_____

_____

_____

_____

What can I start to do today?

My topic:

_____

_____

_____

_____

_____

_____

_____

_____

_____

_____

_____

_____

_____

_____

_____

What do I do today that I need to keep doing?

_____

_____

_____

_____

_____

_____

_____

_____

_____

_____

_____

_____

_____

What do I do today that I need to stop doing?

_____

_____

_____

_____

_____

_____

_____

_____

_____

_____

_____

_____

_____

What can I start to do today?

_____

_____

_____

_____

_____

_____

_____

_____

_____

_____

_____

_____

_____

_____

My topic:

_____

_____

_____

_____

_____

_____

_____

_____

_____

_____

_____

_____

_____

_____

_____

What do I do today that I need to keep doing?

_____

_____

_____

_____

_____

_____

_____

_____

_____

_____

_____

_____

_____

What do I do today that I need to stop doing?

_____

_____

_____

_____

_____

_____

_____

_____

_____

_____

_____

_____

_____

_____

_____

What can I start to do today?

_____

_____

_____

_____

_____

_____

_____

_____

_____

_____

_____

_____

_____

My topic:

_____

_____

_____

_____

_____

_____

_____

_____

_____

_____

_____

_____

_____

_____

_____

What do I do today that I need to keep doing?

_____

_____

_____

_____

_____

_____

_____

_____

_____

_____

_____

_____

_____

What do I do today that I need to stop doing?

_____

_____

_____

_____

_____

_____

_____

_____

_____

_____

_____

_____

What can I start to do today?

_____

_____

_____

_____

_____

_____

_____

_____

_____

_____

_____

_____

_____

_____

Reflection: How do I expose myself to new and inspiring ideas to keep developing?

_____

_____

_____

_____

_____

_____

_____

_____

_____

_____

_____

_____

Reflection: How do I keep my current motivation?

My topic:

_____

_____

_____

_____

_____

_____

_____

_____

_____

_____

_____

_____

_____

_____

_____

_____

What do I do today that I need to keep doing?

What do I do today that I need to stop doing?

_____

_____

_____

_____

_____

_____

_____

_____

_____

_____

_____

_____

_____

_____

What can I start to do today?

_____

_____

_____

_____

_____

_____

_____

_____

_____

_____

_____

_____

_____

_____

My topic:

_____

_____

_____

_____

_____

_____

_____

_____

_____

_____

_____

_____

_____

_____

_____

What do I do today that I need to keep doing?

_____

_____

_____

_____

_____

_____

_____

_____

_____

_____

_____

_____

_____

_____

What do I do today that I need to stop doing?

_____

_____

_____

_____

_____

_____

_____

_____

_____

_____

_____

_____

_____

What can I start to do today?

_____

_____

_____

_____

_____

_____

_____

_____

_____

_____

_____

_____

_____

_____

My topic:

_____

_____

_____

_____

_____

_____

_____

_____

_____

_____

_____

_____

_____

_____

_____

What do I do today that I need to keep doing?

What do I do today that I need to stop doing?

_____

_____

_____

_____

_____

_____

_____

_____

_____

_____

_____

_____

_____

_____

What can I start to do today?

_____

_____

_____

_____

_____

_____

_____

_____

_____

_____

_____

_____

_____

_____

My topic:

_____

_____

_____

_____

_____

_____

_____

_____

_____

_____

_____

_____

_____

What do I do today that I need to keep doing?

_____

_____

_____

_____

_____

_____

_____

_____

_____

_____

_____

_____

_____

What do I do today that I need to stop doing?

What can I start to do today?

_____

_____

_____

_____

_____

_____

_____

_____

_____

_____

_____

_____

_____

My topic:

_____

_____

_____

_____

_____

_____

_____

_____

_____

_____

_____

_____

_____

_____

What do I do today that I need to keep doing?

_____

_____

_____

_____

_____

_____

_____

_____

_____

_____

_____

_____

What do I do today that I need to stop doing?

_____

_____

_____

_____

_____

_____

_____

_____

_____

_____

_____

_____

_____

_____

What can I start to do today?

Reflection: How do I expose myself to new and inspiring ideas to keep developing?

_____

_____

_____

_____

_____

_____

_____

_____

_____

_____

_____

_____

_____

Reflection: How do I keep my current motivation?

My topic:

_____

_____

_____

_____

_____

_____

_____

_____

_____

_____

_____

_____

_____

_____

_____

_____

What do I do today that I need to keep doing?

_____

_____

_____

_____

_____

_____

_____

_____

_____

_____

_____

_____

_____

What do I do today that I need to stop doing?

_____

_____

_____

_____

_____

_____

_____

_____

_____

_____

_____

_____

_____

_____

What can I start to do today?

_____

_____

_____

_____

_____

_____

_____

_____

_____

_____

_____

_____

_____

My topic:

_____

_____

_____

_____

_____

_____

_____

_____

_____

_____

_____

_____

_____

_____

What do I do today that I need to keep doing?

What do I do today that I need to stop doing?

_____

_____

_____

_____

_____

_____

_____

_____

_____

_____

_____

_____

What can I start to do today?

My topic:

_____

_____

_____

_____

_____

_____

_____

_____

_____

_____

_____

_____

_____

_____

_____

What do I do today that I need to keep doing?

_____

_____

_____

_____

_____

_____

_____

_____

_____

_____

_____

_____

_____

What do I do today that I need to stop doing?

_____

_____

_____

_____

_____

_____

_____

_____

_____

_____

_____

_____

_____

What can I start to do today?

My topic:

_____

_____

_____

_____

_____

_____

_____

_____

_____

_____

_____

_____

_____

_____

_____

What do I do today that I need to keep doing?

What do I do today that I need to stop doing?

_____

_____

_____

_____

_____

_____

_____

_____

_____

_____

_____

_____

_____

_____

What can I start to do today?

_____

_____

_____

_____

_____

_____

_____

_____

_____

_____

_____

_____

_____

My topic:

_____

_____

_____

_____

_____

_____

_____

_____

_____

_____

_____

_____

_____

_____

_____

_____

What do I do today that I need to keep doing?

What do I do today that I need to stop doing?

_____

_____

_____

_____

_____

_____

_____

_____

_____

_____

_____

_____

_____

_____

What can I start to do today?

Reflection: How do I expose myself to new and inspiring ideas to keep developing?

_____

_____

_____

_____

_____

_____

_____

_____

_____

_____

_____

_____

Reflection: How do I keep my current motivation?

_____

_____

_____

_____

_____

_____

_____

_____

_____

_____

_____

_____

_____

My topic:

What do I do today that I need to keep doing?

What do I do today that I need to stop doing?

_____

_____

_____

_____

_____

_____

_____

_____

_____

_____

_____

_____

_____

What can I start to do today?

My topic:

_____

_____

_____

_____

_____

_____

_____

_____

_____

_____

_____

_____

_____

_____

What do I do today that I need to keep doing?

_____

_____

_____

_____

_____

_____

_____

_____

_____

_____

_____

_____

_____

What do I do today that I need to stop doing?

_____

_____

_____

_____

_____

_____

_____

_____

_____

_____

_____

_____

_____

What can I start to do today?

_____

_____

_____

_____

_____

_____

_____

_____

_____

_____

_____

_____

_____

My topic:

What do I do today that I need to keep doing?

What do I do today that I need to stop doing?

What can I start to do today?

My topic:

_____

_____

_____

_____

_____

_____

_____

_____

_____

_____

_____

_____

_____

_____

_____

_____

What do I do today that I need to keep doing?

_____

_____

_____

_____

_____

_____

_____

_____

_____

_____

_____

_____

What do I do today that I need to stop doing?

_____

_____

_____

_____

_____

_____

_____

_____

_____

_____

_____

_____

_____

What can I start to do today?

My topic:

What do I do today that I need to keep doing?

_____

_____

_____

_____

_____

_____

_____

_____

_____

_____

_____

_____

What do I do today that I need to stop doing?

What can I start to do today?

_____

_____

_____

_____

_____

_____

_____

_____

_____

_____

_____

_____

Reflection: How do I expose myself to new and inspiring ideas to keep developing?

Reflection: How do I keep my current motivation?

_____

_____

_____

_____

_____

_____

_____

_____

_____

_____

_____

_____

_____

My topic:

_____

_____

_____

_____

_____

_____

_____

_____

_____

_____

_____

_____

_____

_____

What do I do today that I need to keep doing?

_____

_____

_____

_____

_____

_____

_____

_____

_____

_____

_____

_____

_____

What do I do today that I need to stop doing?

_____

_____

_____

_____

_____

_____

_____

_____

_____

_____

_____

_____

_____

What can I start to do today?

_____

_____

_____

_____

_____

_____

_____

_____

_____

_____

_____

_____

_____

My topic:

_____

_____

_____

_____

_____

_____

_____

_____

_____

_____

_____

_____

_____

_____

_____

What do I do today that I need to keep doing?

_____

_____

_____

_____

_____

_____

_____

_____

_____

_____

_____

_____

_____

What do I do today that I need to stop doing?

What can I start to do today?

_____

_____

_____

_____

_____

_____

_____

_____

_____

_____

_____

_____

_____

_____

My topic:

_____

_____

_____

_____

_____

_____

_____

_____

_____

_____

_____

_____

_____

_____

What do I do today that I need to keep doing?

What do I do today that I need to stop doing?

_____

_____

_____

_____

_____

_____

_____

_____

_____

_____

_____

_____

What can I start to do today?

My topic:

_____

_____

_____

_____

_____

_____

_____

_____

_____

_____

_____

_____

_____

_____

What do I do today that I need to keep doing?

_____

_____

_____

_____

_____

_____

_____

_____

_____

_____

_____

_____

_____

What do I do today that I need to stop doing?

_____

_____

_____

_____

_____

_____

_____

_____

_____

_____

_____

_____

_____

What can I start to do today?

_____

_____

_____

_____

_____

_____

_____

_____

_____

_____

_____

_____

My topic:

What do I do today that I need to keep doing?

What do I do today that I need to stop doing?

What can I start to do today?

_____

_____

_____

_____

_____

_____

_____

_____

_____

_____

_____

_____

_____

Reflection: How do I expose myself to new and inspiring ideas to keep developing?

_____

_____

_____

_____

_____

_____

_____

_____

_____

_____

_____

_____

Reflection: How do I keep my current motivation?

_____

_____

_____

_____

_____

_____

_____

_____

_____

_____

_____

_____

_____

My topic:

_____

_____

_____

_____

_____

_____

_____

_____

_____

_____

_____

_____

_____

_____

What do I do today that I need to keep doing?

_____

_____

_____

_____

_____

_____

_____

_____

_____

_____

_____

_____

_____

What do I do today that I need to stop doing?

_____

_____

_____

_____

_____

_____

_____

_____

_____

_____

_____

_____

_____

What can I start to do today?

_____

_____

_____

_____

_____

_____

_____

_____

_____

_____

_____

_____

_____

My topic:

What do I do today that I need to keep doing?

_____

_____

_____

_____

_____

_____

_____

_____

_____

_____

_____

_____

_____

What do I do today that I need to stop doing?

_____

_____

_____

_____

_____

_____

_____

_____

_____

_____

_____

_____

_____

What can I start to do today?

_____

_____

_____

_____

_____

_____

_____

_____

_____

_____

_____

_____

My topic:

_____

_____

_____

_____

_____

_____

_____

_____

_____

_____

_____

_____

_____

_____

What do I do today that I need to keep doing?

What do I do today that I need to stop doing?

_____

_____

_____

_____

_____

_____

_____

_____

_____

_____

_____

_____

_____

What can I start to do today?

_____

_____

_____

_____

_____

_____

_____

_____

_____

_____

_____

_____

_____

My topic:

_____

_____

_____

_____

_____

_____

_____

_____

_____

_____

_____

_____

_____

_____

What do I do today that I need to keep doing?

_____

_____

_____

_____

_____

_____

_____

_____

_____

_____

_____

_____

_____

What do I do today that I need to stop doing?

_____

_____

_____

_____

_____

_____

_____

_____

_____

_____

_____

_____

_____

_____

What can I start to do today?

_____

_____

_____

_____

_____

_____

_____

_____

_____

_____

_____

_____

_____

_____

My topic:

_____

_____

_____

_____

_____

_____

_____

_____

_____

_____

_____

_____

_____

What do I do today that I need to keep doing?

_____

_____

_____

_____

_____

_____

_____

_____

_____

_____

_____

_____

What do I do today that I need to stop doing?

_____

_____

_____

_____

_____

_____

_____

_____

_____

_____

_____

_____

_____

_____

What can I start to do today?

_____

_____

_____

_____

_____

_____

_____

_____

_____

_____

_____

_____

_____

Reflection: How do I expose myself to new and inspiring ideas to keep developing?

_____

_____

_____

_____

_____

_____

_____

_____

_____

_____

_____

_____

Reflection: How do I keep my current motivation?

_____

_____

_____

_____

_____

_____

_____

_____

_____

_____

_____

_____

_____

Well done! You've just completed 50 different thoughts regarding changes in your life and behavior.

What if everybody, each and every one of us, would change 50 things each, where each thing, big or small, makes the world a better place!

I am grateful for your contribution!

Pat yourself on the shoulder and be proud of the work you have done and the contribution you have made!

Bonus mission

Who can I inspire to make changes in their life?

_____

When can you inspire this amazing person to make changes?

_____

How can you inspire this amazing person to make the changes?

_____